T0002467

GROUND BREAKERS

BLACK MUSICIANS

JIMI HENDRIX

by Joyce Markovics

CHERRY LAKE PRESS
Ann Arbor, Michigan

CHERRY LAKE PRESS

Published in the United States of America by Cherry Lake Publishing
Ann Arbor, Michigan
www.cherrylakepublishing.com

Reading Adviser: Beth Walker Gambro, MS, Ed., Reading Consultant, Yorkville, IL
Content Adviser: Michael Kramer, PhD, Music Historian
Book Designer: Ed Morgan

Photo Credits: © Allstar Picture Library Ltd/Alamy Stock Photo, cover and title page; © Pictorial Press Ltd/Alamy Stock Photo, 5; © Gigi Campanile/Shutterstock, 6; Wikimedia Commons, 7; Wikimedia Commons/Heinrich Klaffs, 7; © Everett Collection Inc/Alamy Stock Photo, 9; Wikimedia Commons, 10 top and bottom; © Usa-Pyon/Shutterstock, 11; Wikimedia Commons, 12; © Pictorial Press Ltd/Alamy Stock Photo, 13; Wikimedia Commons/Ilanv, 14; Wikimedia Commons, 15; Wikimedia Commons/Woodstock Whisperer, 16; © MediaPunch Inc/Alamy Stock Photo, 17; © spatuletail/Shutterstock, 18; © Shutterstock, 19; © World History Archive/Alamy Stock Photo, 21; freepik.com, 22.

Copyright © 2024 by Cherry Lake Publishing Group

All rights reserved. No part of this book may be reproduced or utilized in any form or by any means without written permission from the publisher.

Cherry Lake Press is an imprint of Cherry Lake Publishing Group.

Library of Congress Cataloging-in-Publication Data

Names: Markovics, Joyce L., author.
Title: Jimi Hendrix / by Joyce Markovics.
Description: Ann Arbor, Michigan: Cherry Lake Publishing, 2023. | Series:
   Groundbreakers: Black musicians | Includes bibliographical references
   and index. | Audience: Grades 4-6
Identifiers: LCCN 2023003456 (print) | LCCN 2023003457 (ebook) | ISBN
   9781668927823 (hardcover) | ISBN 9781668928875 (paperback) | ISBN
   9781668930342 (ebook) | ISBN 9781668931820 (pdf) | ISBN 9781668933305
   (kindle edition) | ISBN 9781668934784 (ebook)
Subjects: LCSH: Hendrix, Jimi—Juvenile literature. | Guitarists—United
   States—Biography—Juvenile literature. | Rock musicians—United
   States—Biography—Juvenile literature.
Classification: LCC ML3930.H45 M39 2023 (print) | LCC ML3930.H45 (ebook)
   | DDC 787.87166092 [B]—dc23/eng/20230125
LC record available at https://lccn.loc.gov/2023003456
LC ebook record available at https://lccn.loc.gov/2023003457

Printed in the United States of America by
Corporate Graphics

Note from publisher: Websites change regularly, and their future contents are outside of our control.
Supervise children when conducting any recommended online searches for extended learning opportunities.

CONTENTS

THIS IS JIMI

Jimi Hendrix rocked the world with his **explosive** sound. As a young man, he taught himself how to play the electric guitar. He created edgy, **original** music that shocked and thrilled fans. In a few short years, Jimi became one of the most influential musicians in history. This groundbreaker redefined rock and roll. He also understood the power of music to transform lives.

> "MUSIC DOESN'T LIE. IF THERE IS SOMETHING TO BE CHANGED IN THIS WORLD, THEN IT CAN ONLY HAPPEN THROUGH MUSIC."
> —JIMI HENDRIX

The great rock-and-roll musician, Jimi Hendrix

Jimi Hendrix is famous for creating new music as he played. This is called improvisation (im-prov-uh-ZEY-shuhn).

EARLY LIFE

Jimi Hendrix was born Johnny Allen Hendrix on November 27, 1942, in Seattle, Washington. His dad, Al, changed his son's name to James, or Jimmy, for short. Al was African American. And Jimmy's mom, Lucille, was part **Cherokee**. She had Jimmy when she was a teenager. Later, Lucille and Al had another son, Leon.

Lucille and Al had a rocky relationship and little money. Making matters worse, Lucille was **dependent** on alcohol. "She used to drink a lot and didn't take care of herself," said Jimmy. Lucille later left the family. Jimmy and Leon were raised by their often-**violent** dad.

Al Hendrix, Jimmy's dad

Seattle, Washington, in the 1950s

When their parents fought, Jimmy and Leon hid in a cupboard. Jimmy held Leon in his arms to comfort him. Jimmy "learned to lock his feelings deep inside," Leon later said.

Jimmy used music to escape from his tough childhood. He loved listening to B.B. King, Muddy Waters, and other blues musicians. Leon remembers Jimmy holding a broom and pretending to play it like a guitar. Jimmy would also try to make music by plucking rubber bands.

B.B. King is a famous blues musician. The blues is a form of music started by Black people. Blues songs are often about life's hardships.

"MAY THE DREAMS OF YOUR PAST BE THE REALITY OF YOUR FUTURE."
—JIMI HENDRIX

When Jimmy was 16, his aunt bought him an **acoustic** guitar. Jimmy taught himself how to play the instrument. "He wasn't ever apart from it," said Leon. The next year, Jimmy got an electric guitar. But it was meant for someone who was right-handed. So left-handed Jimmy flipped the guitar upside down to play it!

Jimmy learned to express his feelings through music.

Jimmy never learned how to read music. Instead, he figured out how to play by listening to every note!

In 1959, Jimmy dropped out of high school. He worked odd jobs to get by and played music. His guitar skills got better. In 1961, Jimmy was **arrested** by cops. He believed he was targeted for being Black. His punishment was going to jail or joining the U.S. Army. Jimmy chose the army.

Jimmy went to Garfield High in Seattle where there were kids of all skin colors.

Jimmy in the U.S. Army in 1961

Jimmy thought of his guitar as a part of himself.

The army was not a good fit for Jimmy. He was unhappy and homesick. Soon, Jimmy sent for his guitar and started playing music again. This cheered Jimmy up, but his army officers were not amused. Jimmy was **discharged** from the army a year early. The discharge report said, "His mind apparently cannot function while performing duties and thinking about his guitar."

Jimmy started writing letters to his dad when he was in the army. And he never stopped.

MAKING MUSIC

Jimmy's army career was over. However, his star was rising. He began touring the country with other Black musicians such as Sam Cooke, Little Richard, and Curtis Mayfield. Jimmy and the other musicians often faced **racism**, especially in the **segregated** South. Even at some gas stations, they weren't allowed to use the same bathrooms as whites.

A poster for a Little Richard concert

"MY GOAL IS TO BE ONE WITH THE MUSIC. I JUST DEDICATE MY WHOLE LIFE TO THIS ART."
—JIMI HENDRIX

At the same time, Jimmy started making records. He kept writing to his dad, who rarely wrote back. "You may hear a record from me. . . . Don't be ashamed," wrote Jimmy. In 1964, Jimmy moved to New York City. Two years later, he formed a band called Jimmy James and the Blue Flames. Not long after, Jimmy moved to London and changed the spelling of his name to *Jimi*. He created a new band there—The Jimi Hendrix Experience.

Jimi with his bandmates from The Jimi Hendrix Experience

The first song The Jimi Hendrix Experience released was "Hey Joe." It became a top-ten hit! More hit songs followed. The music was a mix of blues, rock, and Jimi's raw vocals. Jimi called his sound "funky freaky." The new band toured the world gaining **popularity**. Their **debut** album—*Are You Experienced?*—came out in 1967. A music **critic** called it "the album that shook the world . . . leaving it changed forever."

That same year, Jimi's band performed at the Monterey International Pop Music Festival. Jimi played and sang his heart out. The audience was stunned by his energy, feeling, and originality. The set ended with Jimi setting his guitar on fire. "You **sacrifice** things you love. I love my guitar," Jimi later said.

At the Monterey International Pop Music Festival, Jimi played his electric guitar with his tongue and teeth! He often played his guitar in unusual ways.

The Monterey International Pop Music Festival lasted 3 days. It was held from June 16 to 18 in Monterey, California. Musicians Janis Joplin and Otis Redding also performed.

Jimi spent the next few years touring with his band. The Jimi Hendrix Experience released two more albums in 1968. One was *Axis: Bold as Love*. The other was *Electric Ladyland*. Critics called this record a masterpiece. Hit singles included "Foxy Lady," "Purple Haze," and "All Along the Watchtower."

The Woodstock Music and Art Fair in Bethel, New York

"DON'T USE YOUR BRAIN TO PLAY IT, LET YOUR FEELINGS GUIDE YOUR FINGERS."
—JIMI HENDRIX

By 1969, Jimi was the highest-paid rock musician in the world. But his life was falling apart. Jimi was abusing drugs and alcohol and working nonstop. In August, he **headlined** at Woodstock, a rock festival in upstate New York. Nearly 500,000 people came. Jimi played a **distorted** version of "The Star-Spangled Banner." Some thought it was a **protest** against the Vietnam War. Jimi said, "I'm American, so I played it." When he left the stage, he fell over from **exhaustion**.

Jimi performing at Woodstock

The United States got involved in a **civil war** in Vietnam (1954–1975). Many Americans disagreed about the nation's involvement in the Vietnam War. Almost 60,000 Americans died in the fighting, including many Black Americans.

Two weeks after Woodstock, Jimi played a free concert in Harlem, a mostly Black neighborhood in New York City. But he was booed on stage. Many Black people thought Jimi played rock music for white people. A disappointed Jimi said, "There is no white or Black rock."

Jimi was proud to be Black and Native American—and, most of all, a human being.

"YOU HAVE TO GIVE PEOPLE SOMETHING TO DREAM ON."
—JIMI HENDRIX

Years of drug and alcohol use and exhaustion finally caught up with Jimi. His band broke up. In 1970, Jimi returned to Seattle to play a show and to see his family. Jimi still wanted his father's love. Once again, Al pushed his son away, even after Jimi bought him a new house. A few weeks later, Jimi was gone.

Jimi with his dad in Seattle

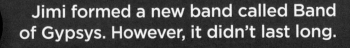

Jimi formed a new band called Band of Gypsys. However, it didn't last long.

JIMI'S IMPACT

On September 18, 1970, Jimi Hendrix died in London after a night of drinking and drugs. He was only 27 years old. Jimi's body was flown to Seattle for his **funeral**. There, Al finally showed Jimi love. Through tears, he moaned, "My son!" Jimi was buried near his mother, Lucille.

Jimi is remembered as one of the greatest guitarists who ever lived. In just 4 years, this self-taught groundbreaker created a **dynamic** new sound. Jimi left a **legacy** that continues to inspire and move people to their souls.

> "WHEN THE POWER OF LOVE OVERCOMES THE LOVE OF POWER, THE WORLD WILL KNOW PEACE."
> —JIMI HENDRIX

In 1992, Jimi was **inducted** into the Rock and Roll Hall of Fame.

GREATEST HITS

Here are some of Jimi Hendrix's signature songs:

Purple Haze

Fire

The Wind Cries Mary

Hey Joe

All Along the Watchtower

Foxy Lady

Bold as Love

Voodoo Child

Fire

Freedom

* Some of these songs include words that might not be appropriate for young people. Please talk to a parent or an adult before listening.